My Christmas Art Class

Nellie Shepherd

DK

DK

LONDON, NEW YORK, MUNICH, MELBOURNE, AND DELHI

Editor Penny Smith
Senior Designer Wendy Bartlet
Additional Design Melanie Leighton
Production Shivani Pandey
Photography Stephen Hepworth

For my brother Stephen Hepworth (A Wonderful Photographer!)

ACKNOWLEDGMENTS
With thanks to: Jean Gollner, Anne Lumb, David Hansel (Memery Crystal),
Joseph Whitworth Centre, Broomhall Nursery School and Early Years
Centre, and all the children who took part in the photography.
Special thanks to the artists: Peggy Atherton, Emma Hardy,
Jane McDonald, Katie Noorlander, and Allie Scott.

First American Edition, 2004
Published in the United States by
DK Publishing, Inc.
375 Hudson Street
New York, New York 10014
04 05 06 07 08 10 9 8 7 6 5 4 3 2 1

A Cataloging-in-Publication record for this book
is available from the Library of Congress.
ISBN: 0-7566-0756-6

Color reproduction by GRB Editrice, Italy
Printed and bound in China by Toppan

Discover more at
www.dk.com

Where to find things

My Christmas Art Class

Here's a book filled with funky, festive things to make at Christmas time.

Yippee, it's Christmas—my favorite time of year! I'd love everyone to have a merry Christmas making things to play with and give away. In this book you'll find fantastic festive decorations, a reindeer headdress, gift-wrapping ideas, a mega pop-up Christmas card, and lots more. Get out your glue and your glitter and go for it!

Love
Nellie x

Read Nellie's Christmas tips on page 46.

Basic kit

As well as the equipment pictured with each project, you will need the following basic kit:

posterboard	glitter
paper	glitter glue
tissue paper	yarn
PVA glue	pom-pons
tape	wiggly eyes
paintbrushes	felt
scissors	
felt-tip pens	
stapler	

Keep your art kit in a box so you can find it easily!

Helping hand

All the projects in this book are designed for young children to make, but they should only be attempted under adult supervision. Extra care should be taken when using sharp equipment, such as scissors, staplers, and pipe cleaners, and with small objects that may cause choking. Only use PVA or other nontoxic, water-soluble glue.

Snowman Sam

winter hat

pillowcase

Here's a little
Snowman
Made from
A pillowcase.
Using bits
Of colored felt,
Stick a smile
Onto his face.

scarf

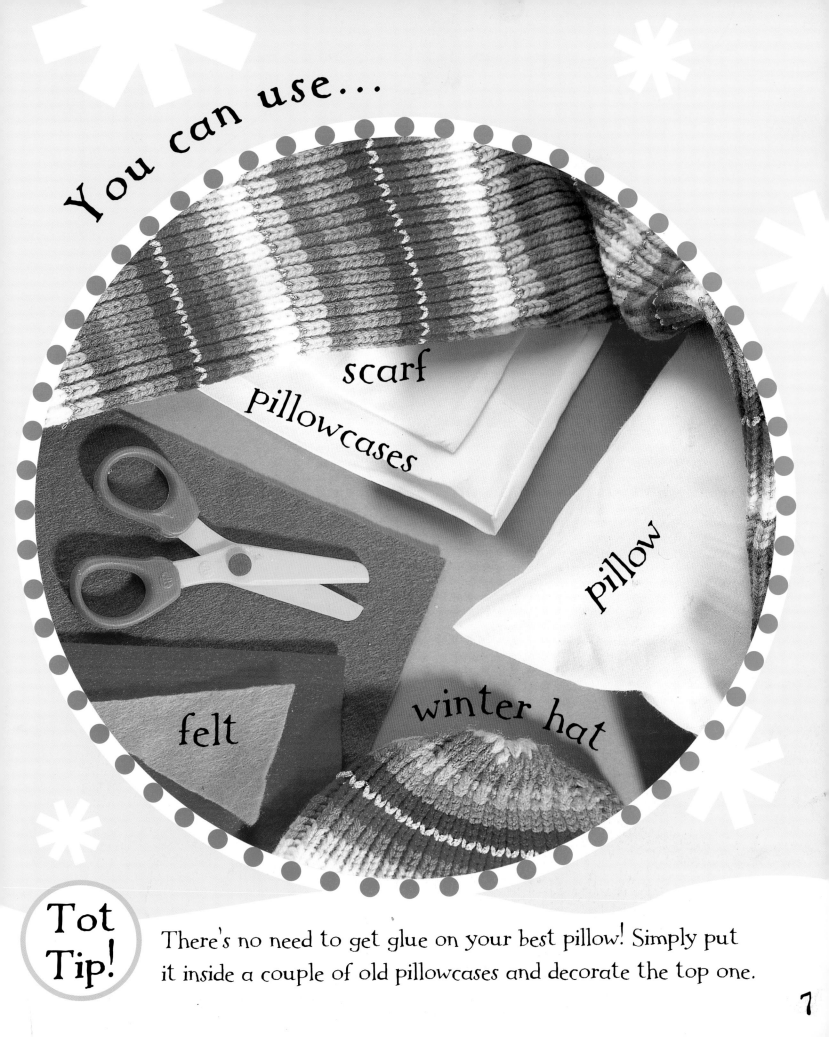

You can use...

scarf

pillowcases

pillow

felt

winter hat

Tot Tip! There's no need to get glue on your best pillow! Simply put it inside a couple of old pillowcases and decorate the top one.

How to make it!

tie

Put your pillowcases on your pillow. Tie a scarf around the pillow to make Snowman Sam's head and body.

cut out

Cut out Sam's felt face—big eyes, pink cheeks, a carrot-shaped nose, and lots of circles for his big smile.

glue

Put a winter hat on Sam's head, then glue on his felt face.

stick

Cut out Sam's felt lapels, buttons, pocket, and holly, and stick them on his body. Now he's ready to cuddle!

I'm soft as snow!

8

Kids' talk
"Snowmen live
outside so they
don't drip on
the carpet."
Tom, age 4

Have a Heart

This lovely heart
Is made from beans.
It can be big or small.
It's the perfect decoration
For your tree or for your wall.

dried kidney beans

paint

ribbon

You can use...

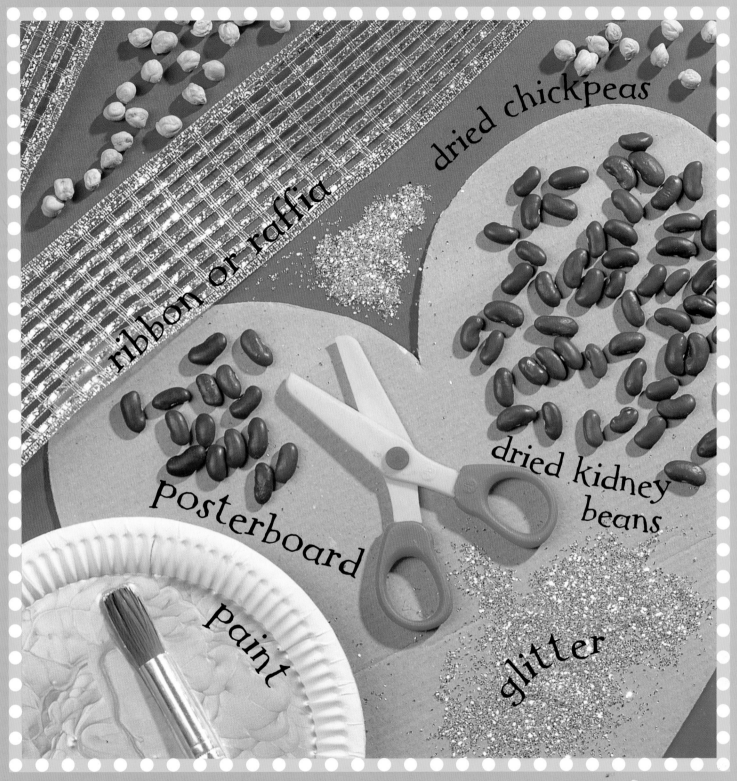

dried chickpeas

ribbon or raffia

dried kidney beans

posterboard

paint

glitter

Tot Tip! Make little hearts to hang on your Christmas tree. You can use dried beans or chickpeas to decorate them.

You can do it!

cut out

I love this decoration—it's so incredibly easy to make! Start by drawing a big heart shape on a sturdy piece of posterboard. Then cut it out.

brush

The next thing to do is to brush a nice, thick layer of sticky glue all over your heart.

place

Place dried beans or chickpeas in the glue, as close together as you can. If you'd like to make a pattern, circles and swirls work really well!

paint

Mix a little glue into your paint. Then paint your heart and sprinkle it with glitter. Glue on a ribbon or raffia bow. Remember to lay your heart flat until it's completely dry.

Kids' talk

"I have a heart and it lives in my tummy."
Georgie, age 4 ¾

Twinkle Star

You're
Dressed as
A sparkling star,
Shining brightly
From afar.
And as you twinkle,
All will see
Just how starlike
You can be.

ribbon

posterboard

14

You can use...

posterboard

tissue paper

glue

kitchen foil

ribbon

glitter

shiny jewels

cellophane

shiny paper

stickers

Tot Tip!

Would you like a wand to go with your outfit? Then cut out a paper star, cover it with glitter, and tape it to the top of a pencil.

15

Here we go!

big star

Draw and cut out a big posterboard star. Decorate it with foil, cellophane, or shiny paper. For extra sparkle, stick on shiny jewels, stickers, or glitter. Staple ribbon to your star so you can hang it around your neck.

star hat

For a star hat, cut a posterboard strip to fit around your head. Decorate it with tissue paper and glitter. Then staple it together at the back.

staple on a star

Add a fabulous shooting star to your hat. Staple a glittery star to one end of a posterboard strip, then staple the other end to your hat.

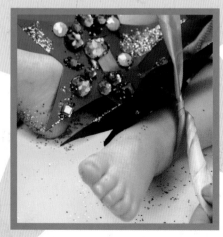

twinkle toes

To brighten up your feet, decorate more stars with glitter and shiny jewels. Thread ribbon through holes in the stars, then tie the stars to your ankles.

16

Kids' talk
"Twinkle, twinkle, little star. How I wonder what you are." Mia, age 3

Rosie Reindeer

My name
Is Rosie Reindeer,
And I pull Santa's sleigh.
I help deliver presents
In time for Christmas Day!

twig

glitter

You can use...

twigs

twigs

tissue paper

glitter

posterboard

staples

card

Tot Tip!

Here's the shape you need for your reindeer headdress. Copy it onto a big piece of posterboard.

How to make it!

cut out

Cut out your reindeer headdress. Make sure it fits comfortably around your head.

sprinkle

To make beautiful antlers, brush glue over a couple of twigs and sprinkle them with glitter.

decorate

Decorate your headdress with little balls of scrunched-up tissue paper, sparkly glitter, paper, or felt.

tape

Tape your antlers to your headdress. To make them extra-secure, tape squares of paper over the ends of the twigs.

staple

Staple your headdress together at the back. Now you can pretend to be Rosie!

Kids' talk

"Reindeers like
Christmas
cookies."
Amy, age 4

Christmas Time!

pipe cleaner

paper star

Here's a
Christmas present.
Doesn't it look fine?
Move its hands
Around its face,
And learn
To tell the time.

tick
tock!

tick
tock!

You can use...

glitter glue

pipe cleaners

paper

paper fastener

stickers

box

tissue paper

glitter

shiny things

Tot Tip! You can buy number stickers from toy stores and craft shops. Or simply write numbers on your clock using felt-tip pens or glitter glue.

23

Here we go!

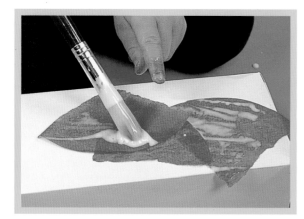

cover

Start making your clock by covering a box with tissue paper. You don't need to be neat—overlapping tissue paper gives a lovely texture.

stick

To make your clock's face, you can stick number stickers on the front of your covered box.

attach

Make two posterboard clock hands. Glue glitter all over them, then attach them to the clock with a paper fastener.

decorate

Decorate your clock with your own gorgeous design of shiny things and glitter glue.

finish

To finish, staple shiny or glittery card stars to pipe cleaners, and push them into the top of your clock.

Kids' talk
"Clocks are smart because they know when it's bedtime."
Joe, age 3 ½

Noël Ninepins

Here's a group of ninepins
Standing straight and tall.
Roll your ball toward them.
Which one's going to fall?

pipe cleaner

I'm a pushover!

cotton balls

You can use...

plastic bottles

tissue paper

cotton balls

wool

glitter glue

Ping-Pong balls

shiny things

Paint

pipe cleaners

crepe paper

fur

stickers

You can do it!

brush

You can copy our pins or design your own. Make one pin at a time. Start by brushing glue over a plastic bottle.

wrap

Wrap crepe paper or cotton balls around your sticky bottle.

I'm knocked out!

stick

Stick on pipe-cleaner wings or antlers, shiny buttons, fur trim, and other decorations made from glitter glue, stickers, tissue paper, or anything you like.

make a head

Make a head for a character pin by cutting a hole in a Ping-Pong ball. Push the ball onto your bottle and paint it.

stick again

Stick or draw a face on the pin. You can make hair from yarn, antlers or a headdress from pipe cleaners, hats from paper, or use whatever is at hand.

Glitter Birds

Put these
Little birds
On the branches
Of your tree.
They'll sit there
All through
Christmas
Sparkling merrily.

tissue
paper

I love to
sparkle!

feather

glitter

You can use...

feathers

wiggly eye

lace

tissue paper

clothespin

posterboard

felt

glitter

Tot Tip!

Each glitter bird has a clothespin taped to the back. You can also tape clothespins to glittery stars or hearts, and pin these to your tree.

Here we go!

draw

Start making a lovely little glitter bird by drawing around a cup on posterboard and cutting it out.

sprinkle

Brush the cut-out with glue and sprinkle on lots of glitter. Shake off any excess.

stick

Now stick on a tissue-paper beak and a wiggly eye. Make your bird's wing from paper, lace, or felt, and its tail from paper or a feather.

tape

Tape a clothespin to the back of your glitter bird. Then put the bird on your Christmas tree.

"Real birds
are fluffy,
not glittery."
Samuel, age 5

Mega Pop-Up Card

pipe cleaner

pop-up fold

fur

tissue paper

This giant Christmas card
Has surprises inside.
Pictures pop up
When you open it wide!

You can use...

pom-pons

glitter glue

doily

feathers

fur

shiny paper

stickers

pipe cleaners

shiny things

tissue paper

posterboard

glitter

Tot Tip! Don't forget to decorate the front of your card! Simple paper shapes, pom-pons, and shiny things are fun to use and look great!

How to make it!

fold

Start making the pop-up part of your Christmas card by folding a big posterboard rectangle into a "W" shape as shown here.

draw

Draw a Christmas tree on the folded posterboard. Cut out your drawing to make four trees attached to each other.

glue

Fold an even bigger piece of posterboard in half. Glue the end Christmas trees inside, so the two middle trees can pop up. Decorate with glitter, stickers, shiny things, and tissue paper.

more pop-ups

You can make hearts or angels in the same way as your trees. Give the angels faces, dresses, arms, and legs using yarn, pipe cleaners, and other odds and ends.

37

Mr. Santa

cotton balls

balloon

This Mr. Santa
Is easy to make.
His tummy is round.
I think he likes cake!

38

You can use...

felt

wiggly eyes

posterboard

cotton balls

paper plate

balloon

sticky-back paper

Tot Tip! Don't be tempted to remove sticky-back paper or tape once you've stuck them to Mr. Santa's balloon body. If you pull them off, he'll pop!

You can do it!

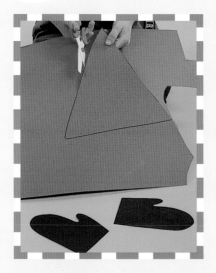

cut out

Cut out the pieces of Mr. Santa—posterboard arms, legs, hands, and feet, and a felt or paper hat. Blow up his balloon body.

fold

Fold Mr. Santa's arms and legs and attach them to his hands and feet. Tape his arms and legs to his balloon body. Dress up Mr. Santa—stick on tissue paper, cotton balls, glitter glue, or sticky-back paper.

tape

For Mr. Santa's head, tape a paper plate to the knot on his balloon body.

glue

Tape Mr. Santa's hat to the paper plate. Then glue on his wiggly eyes, paper mouth, and a nose made from paper or a pom-pon. Finally, stick on his cotton beard and hair.

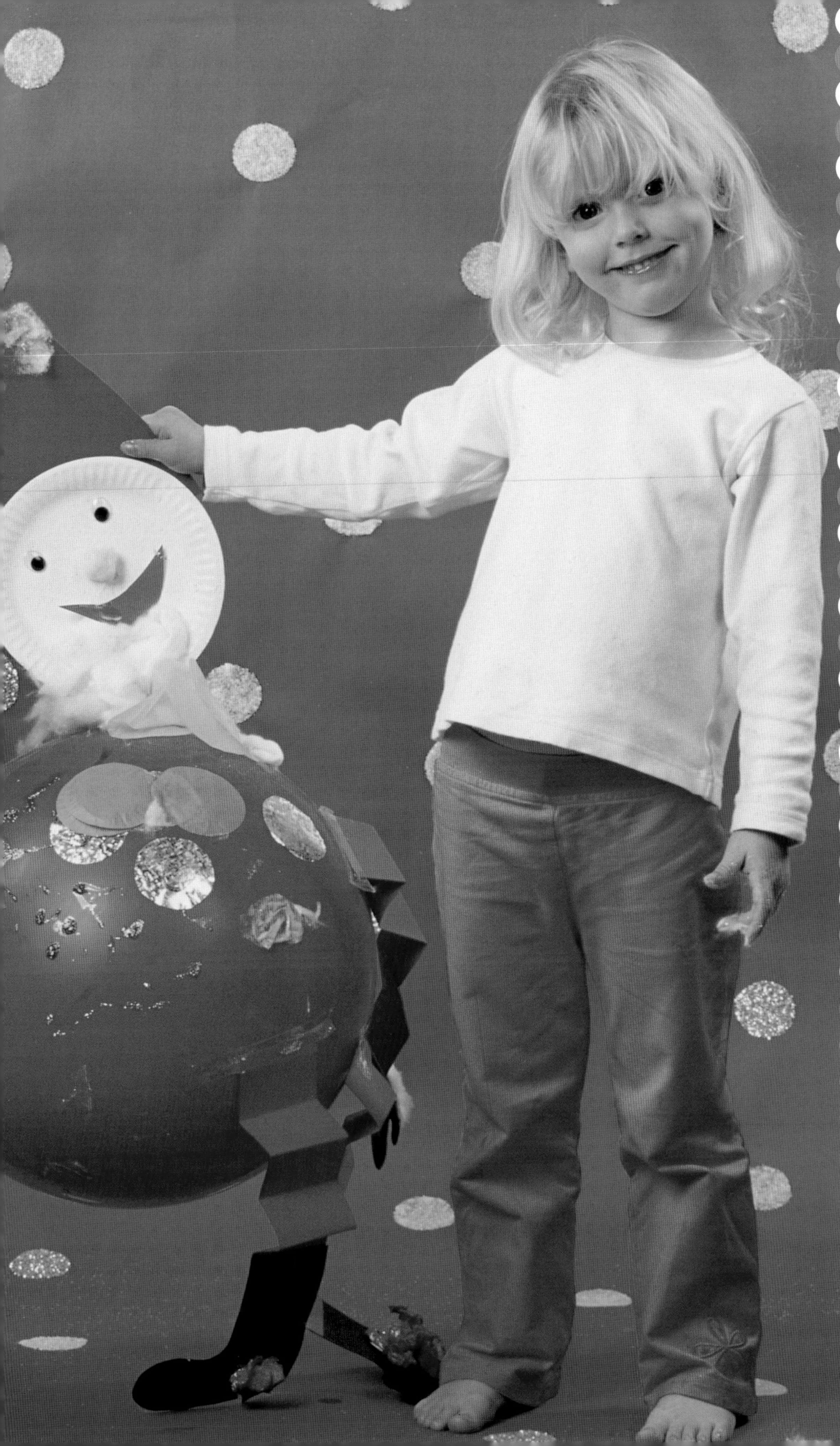

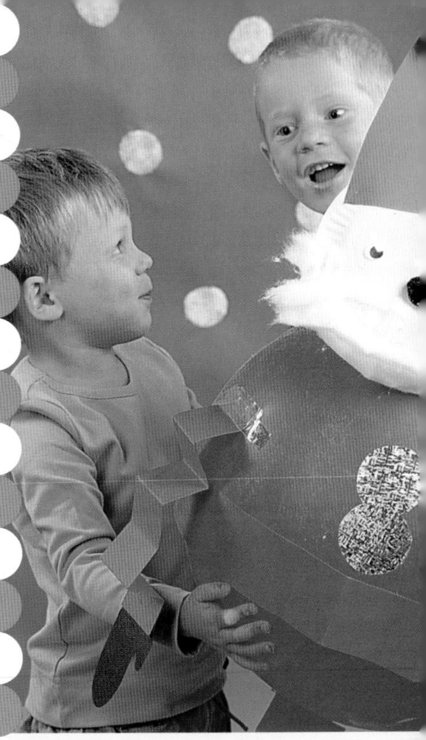

Kids' talk

"Mr. Santa's big, but not as big as my daddy."
Elena, age 5

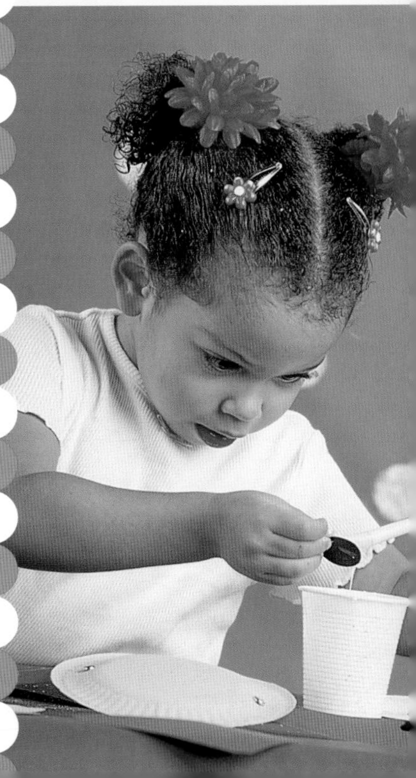

It's a Wrap!

Dress up your Christmas presents
With paper and gift tags, too.
Put them under the Christmas tree
Then see if there's one for you!

fur

paper

You can use...

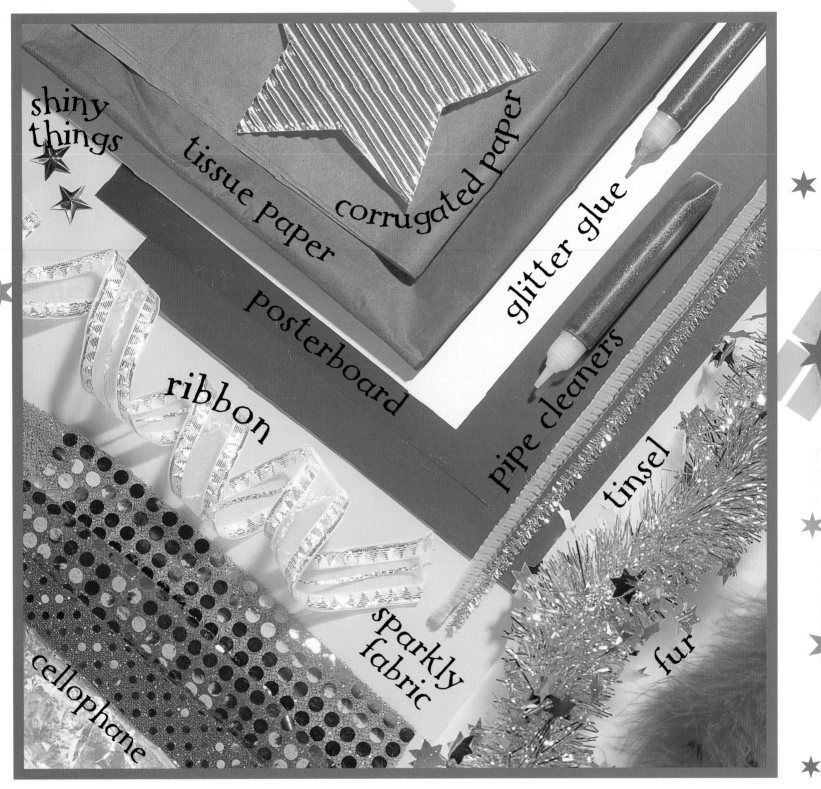

shiny things

tissue paper

corrugated paper

glitter glue

posterboard

ribbon

pipe cleaners

tinsel

sparkly fabric

fur

cellophane

Tot Tip! Look for plastic or fabric Christmas decorations at the store. They look great tied to presents, and you can put them on your tree when everything's unwrapped.

Here we go!

wrapping up

You can wrap your presents in all sorts of lovely things—cellophane, tissue paper, sparkly fabric, or fur. Then tie ribbon or tinsel around them. Tie on unbreakable Christmas decorations, too!

gift tag

To make a fancy gift tag, cut a butterfly shape out of posterboard. Decorate it with tissue paper and glitter glue and wrap a pipe cleaner around the middle, then tie it to a present.

stick-on pictures

Make your presents extra-special by sticking on gorgeous pictures. Try making a fruitcake from corrugated paper. You can decorate it with paper shapes or anything shiny. It looks good enough to eat!

"I wish it could
be Christmas
every day."
Emma, age 4 ¼

45

Nellie's knowledge

Christmas is a time for giving, and children love it when you give them your time. What better way to do this than to spend quality time creating Christmas treasures together?

Making decorations, keeping them safe, and putting them up year after year is a lovely way to bring back happy memories. It also teaches children to respect and care for things.

The joy of giving is something children can experience when they give a gift they've made themselves. It's a fantastic way for them to share their creativity with you.

Valuable presents don't have to cost a fortune. I made my mom a vase 25 years ago. She was so delighted when I gave it to her, and it has always been one of her great treasures!

Praise the presents and Christmas decorations children make. Telling children how brilliantly they've done is so good for all-around confidence.

Recycle your Christmas by making things out of boxes! Empty chocolate boxes and discarded packaging are great for children to recycle and transform.

Display your Christmas cards by hanging them on lines of ribbon. Or stick the cards on boxes, stacked one on top of another, to make a Christmas-card tree!

Refill your art kit with the ribbons, wrapping paper, and shiny odds and ends left over from presents.

New Year calendars are really useful. You can use your recycled bits and pieces to make a collage, and buy a little flip calendar to attach to your design.

Have a fun Christmas. Goodbye!